Manage
12 e

Joan Tunstall is a computer consultant and writer who has worked in the computer industry for over 25 years. Joan believes that while it helps to be computer literate in the modern office, it takes good time management skills to be really effective.

Also by Joan Tunstall:
Easy Email

Manage your time in 12 easy steps

Joan Tunstall

ALLEN & UNWIN

First published in 2000

Copyright © Joan Tunstall 2000

Allen & Unwin
9 Atchison Street
St Leonards NSW 2065
Australia
Phone: (61 2) 8425 0100
Fax: (61 2) 9906 2218
Email: frontdesk@allen-unwin.com.au
Web: http://www.allen-unwin.com.au

National Library of Australia
Cataloguing-in-Publication entry:

Tunstall, Joan.
  Manage your time in 12 easy steps.

  ISBN 1 86508 295 3.

  1. Time management. 2. Success in business.
  I. Title.

650.1

Set in 10.5/14 pt Tiepolo Book by Bookhouse, Sydney
Printed by Australian Print Group, Maryborough, Vic.

10 9 8 7 6 5 4 3 2 1

Contents

How this book can help you

Longer hours have become the hallmark of business today. It's tempting to look back on an era when there were more people to do the job and feel resentment that this is gone. But you don't need to be discontented or drawn into ever-increasing work hours. You can complete your work within your working day simply by managing your time better.

It's not possible to save time—it's only possible to spend your time wisely. This book has plenty of practical tips and hints to help you to make more of each working hour—methods used by people who know how to get the most out of each day. Everyone has the same amount of time in a day, even heads of government or the top managers in your corporation. Some people seem to achieve so much while others achieve so little in the same length of time.

There are old habits to change and new habits to introduce in the quest to use your time wisely. This book encourages you to do so steadily, step by step, making the small important changes that can work together to big effect.

Most time management books start with planning a daily schedule. Sadly, telling a person who is strapped for time and flailing about in daily disorganisation that the most important thing is scheduling is like telling an overweight person that the best way to lose weight is to exercise every day. The overweight person wails, 'I'm too heavy to exercise, let me slim down first'. And so the slimming books start in a different place and work up to a daily exercise routine. So too this book starts in a different place and works up to daily scheduling. By the time you reach it, you should have made enough small changes to have room to fit in those all-important scheduling decisions.

Each chapter of this book represents a step in your progress towards managing your time better. The steps focus on particular aspects of working in business. You will find steps for taming the telephone, pruning your paperwork, clearing the clutter, delegating duties and so forth. Each one is loaded with ideas on how to attack the particular problem—too many changes for you to take on at once.

This is the suggested approach:

1 Read or browse through the whole book if you wish.
2 Now turn to Step 1, the first of 12 easy steps, and read and consider the ideas presented.
3 Pick one thing to do from the step—a thing that you are willing to change and that you think will make a difference.
4 Write down what you have decided and how you are going to apply it to your particular situation.
5 Work actively on applying your decision over the next week. Try to establish it as a new and better habit.

6 At the end of the week assess your progress and feel a sense of achievement.

7 Are you ready to take on something extra? Move on to the next step and do the same. Working on each step in turn will help you to improve your time management in many areas. However, skip steps that don't apply to you and after a while you may like to return to your biggest problem areas and try some extra ideas.

After 12 easy steps you will notice the difference —less stress, more leisure, better balance and a feeling of success. These are all within your reach if you start now.

Knowing where you are going

To manage your time better, the best place to start is admitting that you can't do it all. When you see there is more than you can fit into a day, you quickly reach the conclusion that you must spend your time on the things that are important.

What is important?

Among the dozens of things that you can fill each day with there are probably only a few that really matter. Keeping your real aims in the forefront of your mind is a powerful tool in helping you to decide where you can cut corners and what requires your full concentration. This doesn't mean the other things don't get done—though sometimes this will happen. What it does mean is that you'll keep them in perspective and give them the level of attention they deserve.

Only you can decide what is important to you and goal setting is a good way for you to do this. Goal setting helps you to examine the various demands on your life to discover which ones matter most.

Setting your goals

Think about what you want to accomplish with your time. You can restrict your thoughts to your work environment only, though it is often helpful to consider your whole life because work and private life tend to inter-act. Look at the short term (over the next few weeks and months) and the longer term (over the next year or two). Write down the ideas as they come to you.

Here are some idea starters for setting your goals:
• What major tasks do I want to get done over the next month, next quarter and next year?

- What single achievement at work would make me feel really satisfied?
- What single thing that I did well would make the boss happy?
- Which accomplishment would give the biggest boost to my career prospects?
- Where do I want my career to be in the next year, or five years?
- Do I need any training to reach my career aspirations?
- How much money would I like to make from my work, and what will I do with it?
- Who are the people who are important to me? What goals do I have in relation to them?
- What leisure activity would give me the most pleasure and enjoyment?
- Are there physical and fitness targets I would like to meet?
- How do I want to advance my spiritual life?
- Are there ways that I can help in my community that would be meaningful to me?

Don't worry if you seem to have written down too many goals, or if some of them look as if they won't work together. Feel free to set challenging goals but do try to be realistic and honest with yourself.

Spend an hour or two concentrating on this exercise or grab a few minutes throughout each day, adding to your list. Either way, get the information written down on paper.

Narrowing your focus

It is easier to carry just a few goals around in your head so you need to reduce your long list to a small number of strong statements. Review your list to see what major themes have emerged. You are likely to notice that some goals are different ways of saying the same thing so you can replace these with a single goal. Others could be grouped into a more encompassing goal.

Aim to reduce your list to about five goal statements (no more than ten). Write down each major goal as a fresh statement. Make it specific, stating what you want to achieve, in what time frame and how you will know it has been accomplished.

Under each major goal, list the tasks that will lead you to accomplish the goal. Again, try to make these concrete and measurable. For example, rather than writing 'Get a better knowledge of accounting', write 'Attend the Basic Accounting seminar in June'.

Checking the value of each goal

Some of the goals you have written may still be little more than wishes. As you consider the value of each goal to you and others, you will begin to get a good sense of the ones you genuinely want to accomplish. Remove, add to or adjust your goals as you work through this value assessment.

Here are some questions to help you assess the value of your goals:

- What benefit will I get from reaching this goal?
- Are there any negative effects that may result from this goal?

- What will happen if I don't reach this goal?
- Who else is affected by this goal? Will it matter to them if I don't achieve it?
- What can stop me achieving this goal?
- If somebody else achieved the same thing would I think they had done something worthwhile?
- Is this goal consistent with the things I value in life?

It is helpful to mark the goals as being of high, medium or low value as you work your way through them.

Examining your goals for conflicts

Conflicting goals and tasks can be the reason why they are not achieved and why you waste time by not focusing on the right activities. If, for example, you ignore a conflict between your job goals and career aspirations you may find yourself attaining neither because you have to make an 'either/or' choice.

Also check for conflicts between what you

want to achieve and what others want of you. Some aspect of your job may seem to be the most interesting and rewarding to you, while your manager has another activity in mind for you to accomplish.

Decide how you are going to manage these conflicts. You may need to eliminate a goal or make it less ambitious. Alternatively, you may be able to develop a strategy that will reduce the conflict.

Looking for supporting goals

One of the best ways to maximise your time is to achieve more than one aim with the same activity. Look for ways for your goals and tasks to support each other. For example, you could advance a fitness target by joining the office touch football team which might also double as networking time with work colleagues.

Prioritising your goals

Finally, number your goals by order of importance. Take into account your value assessment, potential goal conflicts and how goals can support each other.

Now, spend a minute or two memorising this order. The ability to recall readily your list of priorities will help you again and again when you have to choose between activities that you might do.

Over the next week

It is best if you can complete this entire goal-setting exercise over the next week. However, if you can't manage this, try considering just one aspect. You might, for example, be aware of a conflict in the things that you are trying to achieve and want to put your thoughts into how you are going to manage that. Or you could actively look for ways that your current activities can support each other. Or you may simply spend time coming to terms with the fact that you can't do it all and decide what you are going to forego.

Whatever you choose, do it throughout this

week, and apply the insight you have gained whenever you have to select between the many activities that can fill your time.

> This week I will . . .
>
> ....
> ....
> ....
> ....

Tracking the time thieves

The things that you think are gobbling your time are often not the real culprits. Guessing intuitively at what needs to be fixed is not the best approach. A more objective measurement is needed to track down the real time thieves.

Why use a tracking sheet?

Filling in a time sheet probably doesn't appeal to you—it doesn't appeal to most people. However, you are encouraged to do so here. The method has been made as painless as possible and you are asked to do it for just one week.

Quite apart from getting an objective measurement of what you are spending your time doing, the act of recording the time for your various activities will help you to develop a better sense of time. You will begin to understand just how long a chatty telephone call can take. You will notice how much time is wasted tinkering with a report that you aren't keen to write. You will be more aware of how often you are interrupted by visitors and how long it takes to return to your work when they are gone.

Even before the exercise is completed, many people find that the act of recording their time usage alerts them to things they hadn't noticed about their work environment and habits. So it's worth trying this exercise even if you can only manage it for one or two days.

Getting started

First, identify up to ten activities that you do. Make a list that suits what you do. You can focus only on work hours, as is done in the example on page 13, or if you prefer you can look across your whole day.

Activities that might be in your working day:
- telephone calls
- correspondence and email
- attending meetings
- reading
- analysis/doing your job
- report writing
- discussion with colleagues/customers
- planning/decision making
- social chat
- travel.

You might prefer to list your activities by the tasks that you do (like entering orders, handling customer complaints). If you choose this method, the goals and tasks that you worked out for Step 1 should be a good guide.

Just for fun, put an asterisk (*) beside the activities that you think are your time thieves. You can check your intuition during the tracking exercise.

Preparing a tracking sheet

Now you are ready to prepare a tracking sheet. Get a blank sheet of paper and list your activities in a column down the left-hand side. Add an extra activity called 'Other' for the small things you have forgotten to list. Across the top put a column for each hour that you work, as shown in Figure 1. Copy your tracking sheet so you have one for each day of the week.

Activity	8	9	10	11	12	1	2	3	4	5	6
Telephone calls											
Correspondence/email											
Attending meetings											
Reading											
Analysis/doing job											
Report writing											
Discussion											
Planning/decisions											
Socialising											
Travel											
Other											

TIME TRACKING SHEET

Time of day

Figure 1 Time tracking sheet

Tracking your time

Every fifteen minutes you are to put a tick ✓ or a cross ✗ against the activity that you did during that interval. Hence, you will have four ticks or crosses in each of the one-hour columns.

Put a tick if you feel that your time was well spent doing that activity. Put a cross when you think that your time could have been spent more appropriately. It might be a good activity but done at the wrong time, or it might simply be the wrong activity for you to have been doing. The goals you set for Step 1 should help you in deciding this.

Some things could be a mixture of time well spent and time wasted. For example, a one-hour discussion with your assistant that you felt went a half-hour too long would be marked as ✓✓✗✗, or a two-hour meeting that started late because someone was missing and descended into fruitless discussion at the end might be marked as ✗✓✓✓✓✓✗✗.

Analysing your findings

Once you have data for a couple of days you can begin analysing it to see what trends emerge.

Questions to help analyse your time usage:

- How much of your day is marked ✗ (time poorly spent)?
- Are you surprised at how your time was allocated?
- Are there big chunks of time that don't contribute to your important goals?
- How much of your day is being controlled by others?
- Is there much time in the 'Other' activity? Is this because you have not correctly identified the activities in your day?
- Were the activities you marked with an asterisk (*) the real time thieves for you?

When your time is not well spent

This section is for the people who found quite a lot of ✗s, indicating that their time could be spent more productively. Try to decide what these represent—good things being done at the wrong time, things that waste time, or good things running overtime. This will indicate whether you need to concentrate more on your priorities or whether there are particular areas, such as pruning your paperwork, from which you will get extra benefit. Pay special attention to the steps in this book that cover your problem areas.

Other things that may be making you less productive:

- procrastination
- delaying decisions
- deadline pressure
- doing things at the last minute
- poor systems and procedures
- chasing people
- lack of resources
- emergencies
- your work environment.

Recognising the problem will help you to do something about resolving it. There are various steps in this book on these topics to help you.

Don't be too concerned if there are times during the day when you are not performing at your peak. It's rare for people to work productively for their whole day. Social chit-chat is fun, makes work enjoyable and can be a useful networking source. You simply need to keep it to an acceptable level.

It's worth noticing whether you have a particular time of day when you are more productive. Some people are best in the morning, others in the afternoon. If you can detect a pattern, schedule your most demanding work at your better time and mundane activities for when you are less alert.

When your time is all well spent

This section is for those who found that their days are almost full of ticks, indicating that nearly all day every day is well spent. You're in a difficult situation if you are not getting all your work done. The first question to ask is whether you've been right in your assessment. It might help to ask other people what they think.

The next thing to consider is the fact that, even though you are working productively, you may not be working on the things that really matter. If you have completed the tracking sheet using functional activities, do it again using a goal-oriented list so that you can confirm whether you are working on high-priority items.

Maybe you are naturally efficient and the time pressure on you is simply because you have too much work to do. If extra help is not going to come your way then you must cut back on lower-priority items, find methods to perform your activities even more efficiently or do things that return more for your effort. You will find suggestions throughout this book that will help you to make small efficiencies that squeeze more into your time.

Another possibility is that you are so efficient that this encourages people to overload you. You might need to say 'No' once in a while.

Over the next week

During this week your aim is to get a proper understanding of how your time is being spent and hence how you can make better use of your time. Remember that it is best not to trust your intuition when it comes to knowing how you are spending your time. This is why you are encouraged to complete a time tracking sheet for at least a couple of days, preferably a whole week.

This week I will . . .

....

....

....

....

Taming the telephone

In this step you will attack one of the most common time thieves—the telephone. The telephone can be a terrific tool, saving both time and energy. However, as every office worker knows, it can also be very intrusive, demanding immediate attention and interrupting the flow of work. You need to achieve a balance between being accessible and being able to concentrate.

Handling incoming calls

While you don't have much control over the arrival of incoming calls, there are some things you can do to reduce their impact on your working day.

How to receive incoming calls more efficiently

- Don't hesitate to say you're busy and then agree on a time when the caller can get back to you.
- Tell the caller of your time constraints—'I can only give you five minutes as I'm due to go out soon.'
- Keep social chit-chat to a polite minimum.
- Have your diary ready to make appointments.
- Record details accurately, confirming telephone numbers and the spelling of names.
- Have your calls screened by an assistant. Keep your assistants well informed so they don't have to interrupt you to satisfy the caller's need.
- Encourage people to talk directly to your assistants rather than trying to contact you.
- If you need undisturbed time then divert calls, turn on the answering machine or take the phone off the hook. If you are waiting for an important call, use call monitoring so you can hear the incoming messages.

Managing your outgoing calls

You only make work for yourself if you place more outgoing calls than necessary, so think before you dial. Don't feel that you have to return every call yourself. If others can handle it, ask them to do so.

How to manage outgoing calls more efficiently

- Plan a time to make outgoing telephone calls in bulk.
- Make the calls in priority order.
- Have at your desk any reference material that you may need during the calls.
- Estimate how long the calls should take and try to keep to this target.
- If the call is going to be complicated, jot down notes before you dial.
- Place your calls at a time when you are fairly sure the people will be available.
- Plan your opening statement while you are waiting for the call to be answered.

▶

- Keep social conversation to a polite minimum.
- When someone talks too much, make an excuse—'I'm sorry, but I have to go to a meeting.'
- If the person you are calling cannot receive your call, agree on a time when you can call back.
- If you are going to be transferred, ask for the name and number of the person you are being transferred to, just in case you are cut off.

Making mobile telephone calls while you are driving can be a time-saving way to set up appointments and clear your backlog of mundane office matters. You will need a 'hands free' device since it is illegal in most jurisdictions to use a hand-held telephone while driving. It's obviously not a great idea to make calls that require you to take notes, refer to papers or concentrate too deeply. Pull over and stop if a call demands concentration.

Stop, too, when you are making important calls because of the potential of poor reception while you are moving.

Consider using email

Use email instead of the telephone. Email has the same friendly feel as a telephone conversation and is growing in popularity because it cuts down on telephone tag, where you and the other person keep missing each other. It also allows you to handle requests at your own convenience rather than interrupting your daily schedule.

Email enables you to think about your reply. It has the added benefit of preserving the information for your records without the need to make file notes. It's also a great way to get a message out to a lot of people at the same time without having to make several telephone calls.

However, email is not a good choice for complicated discussions that require a lot of back and forth questioning. It's faster to make a telephone call and get it finished in one go. Also, never use email for something that requires conversational feedback or tone of voice to soften the impact. Angry and indiscreet email messages have been the source of much embarrassment for many people.

Organising yourself for telephone efficiency

Here are a few extra tips to help you to organise for telephone efficiency.

Keep a telephone log. Loose notes get lost and you waste time looking for the right one among the many that can soon clutter your desk. Have a notebook that you keep beside the telephone to take notes, names and telephone numbers.

Have a pen handy. Pens disappear so easily that it's best to have a distinctive pen in a holder near your telephone so that you and others are less inclined to take it away.

Maintain your telephone directories. Keep your personal address book, business card folder or electronic address book up to date and well organised so that telephone numbers can be found quickly. Have telephone directories nearby, or know how to access them on your computer system.

Know your telephone. Telephone systems today can be very sophisticated and using the features properly can help you to work more efficiently. Unfortunately, the command sequences are sometimes hard to remember, so get the manual for your system and learn the features that are going to help you the most. Keep a command summary beside your telephone until you have used the features often enough to remember them.

Communicate clearly. Get your thoughts together so that you can communicate fully and clearly. There will then be less need for follow-up telephone calls.

Smile. The other person can't see your smile or your hand gestures but it might surprise you how much these things transfer into your voice, so do them anyway. If you are feeling tired, stand up—it will not only keep you fitter, it will give your voice more life.

Use a speakerphone or headset. If you need your hands free to do work while you are on the telephone, you will find it's more efficient to have a telephone with a speaker. However, be aware that speakerphones can be loud and intrusive for others sharing your office so you may need to invest in a headset.

Make conference calls. Conference calls allow people to talk as a group rather than you acting as a go-between. They can also reduce the need for people to spend time travelling.

Over the next week

Choose just a few ways in which you are going to practise taming the telephone this week. And, most of all, keep in mind the goals you set last week so that you make unimportant calls very brief and give quality time to those that matter.

This week I will . . .

....

....

....

....

Pruning your paperwork and email

Stroll around your office and look at the in-trays. There are sure to be more than a few spilling over with papers. Many of the people who own these in-trays also have a guilty stash of more unread papers out of sight in a drawer, cupboard or briefcase. And there is the electronic mailbox, a hidden in-tray, bulging with unread and unprocessed messages. If you are suffering a chronic case of correspondence overload you may be sure that you are not alone. To get on top of it you have two choices—either get rid of it or process it faster.

Clear your in-tray daily

You will handle your paperwork better if you set aside a period each day when you concentrate and give it your full attention, rather than working on it randomly. You should aim to clear both your paper-based and electronic in-trays daily. Reading a letter and then leaving it in your in-tray to be shuffled around again and again is the single most wasteful thing you can do with it.

Resolve to process each item only once. As soon as you have read it, act on it. Decide to do one of four things:

- Throw it away.
- File it for reading or action at a more suitable time.
- Pass it on.
- Process it.

Scan the items quickly—read the title, read the first paragraph, if necessary read the first lines of key paragraphs. This should give you enough to decide what action you should take.

A common trap is to give every item the same amount of attention. What you should do is decide on the importance of the item and act accordingly. Process to immediate completion only the important ones according to your goals and plan for the day.

Cutting off the flow

Junk mail is easy to spot and easy to throw away without feeling guilty. But even this small amount of handling takes time. Cut off the flow of junk mail (if you can) and you will have the immediate satisfaction of your in-tray being less full.

You may have other useless reading material that doesn't look like junk mail. Are you receiving magazines, minutes of meetings, copies of memos and such like, which give you no benefit for the effort of reading them? If so, ask to be removed from the distribution lists and cancel subscriptions to unhelpful magazines.

Junk email messages are a growing problem because it is easy and inexpensive to distribute to a large number of people via email. If the junk messages are coming from an individual, ask them to stop copying you on their email messages. However, it may be a case of your name being on a company distribution list or, worse still, on an unscrupulous outsider's list. Your email administrator or computer help desk can assist you to understand the source of the messages and guide you on how to remove your address from the distribution list.

Reading faster

Another way through the pile of information is to read it more quickly. Try these methods to help you to read faster.

How to read faster
- Skim—look at the headings, illustrations and summaries.
- Concentrate—don't try to read and do something else.

▶

- Keep going forward; back-skipping wastes time.
- Move your eyes faster.
- Push yourself to develop your skill.
- When you are trying to assimilate new material:
  - Don't try to do too much at once.
  - Build up a picture or summary in your mind.
  - Review it each day for two to three days.
  - Put it into use as soon as you can.

Enlisting the help of others

You can save time by enlisting the help of others. If it's not your responsibility to process an item, pass it on. This removes it from your in-tray.

If you have an assistant it is faster to dictate than to write or type a letter. Alternatively, you can write margin notes for the assistant to do the reply.

Have someone throw out junk mail, or scan it so as to provide you with only what seems useful. They can also help by reading information and marking the main points. Another way to get people to help is to ask them to produce summaries for longer documents whenever this is possible.

Write replies only when you have to

Be aware that writing letters and email messages can be compelling as it gives you a warm sense of a task being complete. Other activities, which may be more important to achieving your goals, don't give this same sense of completion. You may find that you are writing unnecessary notes and replies as a means of putting off other tasks. It's worth a moment's thought to see if this is the case with you.

Sometimes there's a quicker way. Could you replace a formal letter with a telephone call or brief email message?

Writing clear messages

People waste time trying to impress others with their writing. Their paragraphs are filled with pompous and unnecessary phrases that are hard to read and understand. You should aim to write clearly in simple conversational language. Here's a good test. Read one of your letters aloud. Did you find yourself reading things that you would never say in person? For example, you might have written 'You will recall that' when in conversation you would simply say 'Remember'.

Try applying the ideas below. These will work for all types of business writing—letters, memos, email messages, meeting minutes and reports.

Write logically

- Jot down the main points and arrange them by importance, putting the most important point first.
- Use these points as the outline for your writing.

Write concisely

- Start with a short informative subject line to encourage the reader to read on.

- In the first paragraph address the key point or summary of the situation. Anything longer than a page should have a summary.
- Use simple conversational language.
- When you have finished, revise and cut. Wordiness irritates readers.

Remember your readers

- Use language the readers will understand. Use abbreviations and jargon only when you know the reader is familiar with the terms.
- Consider how your letter will be seen through their eyes. Does it use the right tone? Is it easy to read?
- Say how you want them to act on this message. Correspondence without a clear action statement usually sits unattended.

Make sure the message is complete

- Ensure that the context is clear. For example, indicate what correspondence you are responding to and which part of it.

- Check that all the information that is needed is included. Time is wasted when people need to come back to you asking for clarification or corrections.

- For a professional finish, check the punctuation and spelling.

Work hard on trying to get your writing right first time. Resist the urge to tinker with your words over and over again to make them perfect. If you have been careful to write clearly from the outset then your correspondence should require little revision.

Writing more quickly

In this age of email and word processors more people are doing their own drafting and typing. Here are some suggestions for getting things done more quickly.

How to write faster
- Write shorter correspondence.

▶

- Find ways to reduce keystrokes—such as using automatic addressing and signatures in email messages.
- Organise your addresses—keep your electronic address books up to date, sort business cards and store them so they can be readily accessed.
- Use templates to provide a standard layout for your correspondence.
- Use form letters and forms to save rewriting the same things again and again.
- Use your business card or a handwritten 'with compliments' slip instead of a cover letter when sending a requested package of material.
- Respond on the back or bottom of the original correspondence. This saves explaining the context. A quick handwritten note is often sufficient. If you need to keep a record, photocopy it before sending.
- Use routing slips.
- Learn the quickest way to do essential activities like spell checking, address lookup and label printing.

▶

- If you are not a touch typist, take a typing course.
- Actively apply clear writing techniques so you can reduce rewriting and become more confident in your own work.

Over the next week

The best thing you can do over the next week is resolve to handle each piece of paper and each email message only once, remembering to keep focused on your priorities. You might also like to choose one or two new methods for getting rid of some of your paperwork or processing it faster.

This week I will . . .

....
....
....
....

Clearing the clutter

If you are the type of person who claims to know exactly what is in each pile of paper toppling at the edge of your desk, then a neat and tidy office may not be your ideal. Even so, it's worth taking an honest look at how your space is organised and making a few changes.

Having too many things around you that clutter your workspace slows you down. Think of the dozens of times you search for a pencil, hunt for a lost document, push aside a pile of paper, or walk to the filing cabinet and say 'Where did I file that?'

Clearing your desk

As your primary working space, your desk is the place to start. Set aside a half-hour or so, sit comfortably in your chair and let the analysis begin. Pick up the items that are on your desktop, one at a time. For each item, decide whether it is serving a useful purpose on your desk. If not, put it away or throw it away.

If your desk is cluttered with documents that need filing, set them aside for a while. The section on designing a better filing system later in this chapter will help you to get that area under control. As part of this exercise, you should aim to have on your desk only documents relating to the task you are currently working on.

Once the desktop is done, start on the drawers. Accumulations of empty ballpoint pens, dried-up markers, obsolete floppy disks and curling notepads only annoy you when you need to find one that works. Again, if the items are serving no useful purpose or have no reason to be close at hand, put them in the cupboard or throw them out.

If you've done this exercise diligently you

may be feeling exhausted, but it's only the start because the real aim is to organise your desk, not just to tidy it.

Organising your office

Sit back in your chair and think about your desk and office space. Decide whether it's working efficiently.

Here are some questions for analysing your office space:

- Do I feel comfortable? Is my chair right for me?
- Are my computer screen and keyboard at the right height and distance?
- Do I have enough space to work?
- Is the lighting bright enough where I am writing or are there shadows over my work? Get a desk lamp if you need it.
- Is the telephone nearby and on the best side of the desk for me? Is the desk diary, pen and paper near it?
- Is the waste-paper basket beside me?

- How often do I walk to the filing cabinet? Could my files be better organised or better placed? Do other people have to interrupt me frequently to get at files stored in my office?

- Is my desk facing in a direction that causes me to be distracted by other activity in the office? It is usually better to place your desk so that you face a wall while working and have to turn away from it to give visitors your full attention.

- Is my work space too noisy or confused? Is there anything I can do to reduce this?

- Do I have a clock so that I am aware of the time? Can my visitors see the clock too?

- Are there things that personalise my space and mark it with my personality? If not, plan to get some.

Now that you have completed your analysis, design a new office and desk layout that improves on at least some of the things that have been found wanting.

Design a better filing system

If you have bulging files, overstuffed filing cabinets, a fear of not being able to find a document again, or you keep coming up against the big dilemma—'Which file should I put it in?'—then you need a better filing system.

There are four commonly used filing methods: alphabetic, subject, numeric and geographic. The method that is right for you depends on the types of documents you handle and how you reference them when you need them again. For example, if you refer back to customer documents and usually work with a customer number rather than a customer name, then numeric filing is probably better. If your documents fall into two broad categories you may need to implement two different filing systems.

Procedure for designing a better filing system
1 Describe the problem.
  • What is to be filed?

- Who else needs access to the files and where are they located?
- How are the files used?

2 Plan your system.
  - Choose your filing method.
  - Select names for the folders. You don't want too few folders or too many.
  - Remember to allow for future expansion.
  - Decide where the files are to be located.

3 Talk it over with others.
  - Get comments from other people who have to share the system.
  - Amend your plan if necessary.

4 Implement your system.
  - Enlist some help or spend a busy weekend.
  - While you are at it, throw out documents that are no longer needed.
  - It helps to write a disposal date on documents when you file them. This makes cleaning up easier in the future.
  - If necessary, train people to use the new system.

▶

5 Evaluate how it is working.

- Remember to get the opinion of others who are using the system too.
- Is it easy to decide where a document belongs?
- Is it easy to find a document when you need it?
- Are the filing cabinets located in the right place?

Schedule periodic cleanup of your files.

If you're afraid to file a document because you might forget it once it's out of sight, then you need an action list, a tickler file or a pending folder—whichever works best for you.

A tickler file has a folder for each day of the month, usually in your desk drawer. File the document on the date when you plan to handle it. Each day, take the tickler file for the day and process the documents in it. Then put the folder at the back. The folder for the next day will then be at the front ready for you to look at tomorrow. If you process your tickler file daily you won't miss doing things, even if you can't handle them immediately.

Another method is simply to make a note on your desk calendar for the day you need to action the item.

Tidying your computer

It's just as important to organise the electronic desktop and filing systems in your computer as it is to organise your physical environment. Make sure you have icons on your desktop (or shortcut bar) for applications that you use frequently. In this way, starting your word processor, getting at your email messages or accessing the Internet is as easy as a single mouse click. At the same time, get rid of clutter from applications that you rarely use. If you don't know how to do this, contact your computer help desk for assistance.

Take a good hard look at how you are filing electronic documents and reorganise the filing system if necessary, using the procedure given earlier for paper documents. The same goes for your email messages. Set up folders for your email messages so it's easy to drop messages into the appropriate folder and easy for you to find them again later.

Spend time learning the extra tricks on your computer that can save you more time in the long run, things like:

- the *Find* command for searching folders for misplaced documents
- filters for automatic filing of email messages
- the task list and calendar to keep your action list and appointments
- the address book for your contacts.

Uncluttering your mind for important tasks

You will work best on difficult tasks if you are able to give them your full attention. Look at the tracking sheets you completed earlier (Step 2) and decide what time of day you are most alert and when you have the best chance of being undisturbed. Plan to do tasks that demand greater concentration at that time of day.

Before you start on a complex task, stand up and stretch to relax your body and clear your mind. Then settle down and concentrate. Building up the ability to concentrate, regardless of the noise and disturbance around you, is like developing physical fitness. Work at it bit by bit and your ability to work solidly on mental tasks will grow.

Over the next week

Plan to unclutter one aspect of your work environment this week—your desk, your office, your filing cabinets, your computer or your mind when doing important tasks.

This week I will . . .

....

....

....

....

Managing meetings

Most people find themselves complaining that they attend too many meetings and that the meetings do not achieve enough for the time spent on them. You need to know how to get through meetings more quickly and how to do without them more often. While there is no single answer to this, there are a few techniques that may help.

Scheduling the meeting

The first thing you should ask when scheduling a meeting is 'Is it necessary?' and then 'Does everyone have to be there?' If people did this more often there would be fewer time-wasting meetings for everyone to attend. It may be possible to arrange your meeting so that some participants have to be there for only part of the time rather than for all of it.

Be considerate of other participants when choosing the time and venue. Try to choose a time that will be convenient to them and least disruptive of their normal workload. Also choose a convenient location.

Set the length of the meeting. Make it just long enough to get the business done. In the notice of your meeting, specify the end time as well as the start time.

Get the meeting notice out well in advance so that people can schedule it in their diaries. If you work with forgetful people remind them closer to the day.

Always prepare and distribute a formal agenda. Use the action list from the previous meeting to create the new agenda. Using the minutes of the previous meeting for the agenda often leads to people covering old ground again.

Circulate papers in advance of the meeting. Indicate that people are expected to read these beforehand. This can save unnecessary presentation of background information during the proceedings.

Managing the meeting

It's the responsibility of everyone present to create a useful and helpful atmosphere. The chair, however, has special responsibility for managing the smooth flow of the discussion, keeping it timely and making it productive.

How to manage meetings more effectively

- Start on time and don't recap for latecomers.
- Stick to the agenda.
- As you move on to each new agenda item, make sure the point of discussion is clearly defined.
- Set a time limit and then open the topic for general discussion.

▶

- Question people to keep the discussion moving. Try to open up the quiet ones but don't go round the table taking input from everyone as this encourages repetition.
- If the discussion strays from the topic, bring it back into focus. If a side topic seems to be fruitful, note it down for later discussion and return to the topic on hand. Be firm with people who are introducing irrelevancies into the discussion.
- Referee if necessary.
- Summarise discussion highlights as you go through.
- Watch the clock and, when the time is up, close the discussion. Stick to the time unless there is a good reason to extend it and participants are agreed that the time should be extended.
- Close the meeting by stating clearly the action items arising from the discussion. An action item is not complete until it covers what is to be done, by whom, how, where and when.

Remember that meetings are meant to be enjoyable, not an endurance test. Schedule breaks, inject humour and control the proceedings amicably, not with a heavy hand.

Participating in meetings

If you are scheduled for a meeting that you feel is unnecessary or poorly organised then challenge it. But if you want the people around you to change, be prepared to lead by example in the meetings that you attend.

How to be a good meeting participant

- Make sure you've done any action items assigned to you.
- Read the background papers before the meeting.
- Turn up on time.
- Bring a notebook, pen and your diary.
- Be willing to explore options.
- Be prepared to put forward your own views clearly and concisely.

▶

- Listen attentively to others.
- If you are the talkative type, hold back a little so others can have a go.
- Try to keep your comments to what is relevant and useful.
- Be flexible; negotiate, compromise and agree so that the action of the meeting can keep moving forward.

When other people are talking, look at their faces and listen instead of beginning to think about your next response or letting your mind wander. If another thought distracts you, make a quick note of it in your notebook and return your attention to the speaker.

Just in case the action list isn't distributed quickly, take a note during the meeting of any actions that affect you.

After the meeting

Encourage those who have contributed to good meeting practice. Spare a moment to thank the chair if the meeting ran well and compliment people who have participated constructively.

Attend to your action items in the agreed time frame. If you were responsible for the meeting, make sure the minutes are written and distributed promptly. At the very least, ensure that the action list is distributed in a matter of days so that people have no excuse for forgetting their action items.

Over the next week

If you have meetings to schedule, attend or chair in the next week, choose one or two things that you can do to make them a more productive and enjoyable experience for everybody who attends.

This week I will . . .

....

....

....

....

REVIEW POINT

You are now midway through the steps for managing your time better. You can probably already notice a difference and you should try to keep up with the new things that you have introduced each week.

- Are you keeping your goals in mind as you make telephone calls, handle paperwork and decide what tasks to spend your time on?

- Are you keeping unimportant telephone calls brief, and are calls causing you less disruption?

- What about the state of your paperwork— do you have it under better control?

- Have you managed to unclutter your work space and kept it that way?

Ending procrastination

There's a job to be done, the deadline is looming and you are not at your desk. Where are you? You're beside the coffee machine, having an extra-long chat interspersed with the comment, 'I should go. I've got this huge job to do and it must be done by tomorrow.' You linger, slowly sipping another cup of coffee. You're procrastinating.

Putting things off until the last minute puts you under extra stress. And feeling guilty because you've put off to tomorrow what you could have done today only makes the condition worse. It's clear—to be on top of things you must put an end to the procrastination and get on with the job.

Reasons for procrastination

There are many reasons why people delay doing tasks that they must eventually complete. In the list below are some of the most common reasons. If you have a task that you've been pushing aside, work out the reason for this.

Why are you procrastinating?

- The task is too big—I don't know where to start.
- It involves something unpleasant—I don't like doing that job.
- Fear of failure—I'm not capable of doing the work.
- Perfectionism—I haven't got time to do it properly so it's best not to begin.
- Pessimism—the job's useless and not worth doing anyway.
- Driven by your emotions—I'd rather wait until I'm in the right mood.
- Worried by criticism—even if I do my best it won't be good enough.

On the other hand, you may have no problem at all with starting but you never seem to finish. Such people always feel they need to do one or two more things to make the job complete, or to make just a few small revisions to give it a final polish, but it never seems quite polished enough. This is just a different form of procrastination, often driven by perfectionism or fear of failure and criticism.

For poor starters

Poor starters can try a number of techniques to get themselves going.

Never wait until you're in the right mood. Feelings are fickle. Most people find that by starting the job their mood settles into tune with the work.

When the task is too big and daunting, break it into smaller pieces. Do each small piece and it won't be long before the whole job is done.

Set some deadlines for yourself. Make trying to meet your targets a game and the whole thing can seem more like fun.

If the job still seems nasty, try doing it as the very first thing in your day and get it out of the way. Remind yourself how much better you're going to feel with it finished. But wait, maybe you don't have to do it at all! There could be some fellow worker who just loves that kind of work and is only too willing to take it on—so delegate it if you can.

Try not to be put off by failure and criticism. Everyone has to go through a learning period and this is your chance to learn. You might even surprise yourself and do better than you thought.

When you have those pessimistic feelings, instead of dallying, write a list of the positive and negative aspects of the job. Go beyond the job itself to the wider benefits. Keep looking until you find something good about it.

Attack the job with enthusiasm. Even if you feel as if you are faking it at the start, your positive attitude will grow on you.

Promise yourself a reward when it is done.

For poor finishers

Poor finishers can give these ideas a try.

Break the job into subtasks and complete each one before you move on. Be hard on yourself, and insist that each step must be completed. Set deadlines and work to them.

If you feel that your work is not quite complete, try to overcome your fear and decide in your heart that it's good enough and move on to the next step. Don't look back. Push yourself to keep going forward.

Remind yourself that the job is no good unless it's finished. Become convinced that all your hard work is to no avail until you reach the end.

Stay unhappy with your progress until the job is completely done.

Decide on your reward for reaching the end.

Evaluating how you are going

Most of these suggestions ask you to change your attitude and that's not easy, so there's a good chance that you won't overcome the problem first time. You can learn from the experience, however, and get better at it each time. Here are some questions to ask yourself whenever you find you're stressing out trying to make another deadline.

The procrastinator's evaluation checklist
- Have I wasted time getting started/finished?
- Why was it so hard to get started/finished?
- How am I going to recognise this and alert myself when it happens again?
- What escape routes have I been using to put off the job?

▶

- What can I do to cut off these escape routes in future?

Over the next week

Don't wait for tomorrow to change your habits. Use today to prepare for a better tomorrow, especially for those tasks that are important to your goals.

This week I will . . .

....

....

....

....

Step 8

Caring for callers

Visitors, both scheduled and unscheduled, can be an exasperating interruption in your daily schedule. And this time thief, unlike others, can seem to be beyond your control because people deserve courtesy even though they can be a major nuisance. You'll be glad to know that there are ways to manage callers in a pleasant and helpful way and still reduce the amount of time they consume.

Being a good listener

Interestingly, one of the best ways to deal with visitors more quickly is to give them more attention. Trying to double up on time by talking to a person while thinking about other things doesn't work. Visitors will know they don't have your attention and will usually slow down.

On the other hand, if you listen intently and show it, they will feel more able to speak and you will hear what they have to say. You'll be able to evaluate what they need more easily and deal with the whole matter more quickly.

Being a good listener

- Do greet your callers warmly, even if you think they're a nuisance.
- Do look at them while they are talking.
- Don't hurry them, even if they are slow at speaking.
- Don't jump to conclusions.
- Do jot down notes.
- Don't let your mind wander to what you're going to say next.
- Do show that you've understood by summarising what you've heard.
- Do guide the speaker with open questions that help get to the heart of the matter and keep them from wandering off the topic.
- Don't get caught up in minor facts and squabbles.

Dealing with drop-in visitors

The visitors with the most potential to disrupt your day are those that drop in without an appointment. Your aim with drop-in visitors is to handle the matter quickly so that you can get back to your scheduled work. Try walking out of your office to meet them so they don't break into your space. If they are already in, then stand so they can't sit. Or you can suggest that they walk with you to another appointment.

As always, listen to them intently so that you understand the matter quickly. If it can't be dealt with easily, make an appointment with the caller to come back at a mutually convenient time. Or say you'll get back to them when you're free—and make sure that you do.

Where you can, encourage people to telephone or use email to contact you instead of this kind of random interruption. However, this will only work if you are good at following up telephone messages and responding to your email. Otherwise, your colleagues have no option but to pop by your office to get your attention and answers to their questions.

Keeping visitors on schedule

It's not just drop-in callers who consume your time—scheduled visitors who are long-winded can be just as troublesome. When people come to your desk they are in your space and unless you exercise control they are going to stop you getting on with other things you have planned for the day. You need to manage the situation so that they don't overstay their welcome but, at the same time, they must feel that they've been given your attention.

The best way to control the length of calls is to set a time limit when the person makes the appointment. When you begin your meeting remind them of your time constraint. But that's the easy part. It's harder sticking to the time limit.

How to keep callers to your time limit

- Schedule meetings in the other person's office rather than your own, then you don't have the problem of getting them out of your space.
- Schedule habitually long-winded callers at times when they will be inclined to leave more quickly—for example, just before lunch or knock-off time or before another meeting they must attend.
- Let staff know of your requirements, such as having a summary and solutions ready to present to you. If callers are unprepared, end the visit and ask them to reschedule when they are prepared.
- Be attentive to your visitors and listen to them.
- Signal to callers when you want the meeting to end: 'Just before you go...', 'Before we finish...'.
- Arrange for your assistant to remind you of your next appointment when the caller's time is up.

▶

- When the time is up, be polite but firm in closing the meeting. Stand up. This sends a clear signal that the meeting is complete.

When a caller is late, let them know when the visit must end. Allowing one appointment to run late can set you back for the whole day. If the person can't finish in the reduced time then reschedule the appointment, unless it's a very important visitor.

Shutting the door

One of the simplest ways to cut off visitors is to shut the door of your office and get an assistant to screen any interruptions that might otherwise occur. However, you mustn't abuse this barrier or you'll get a reputation for being unapproachable and people will begin to storm their way through it anyway. Keep the 'closed door' for times when you really do need to concentrate and be un-disturbed.

If you work in an open-plan office where there are no doors to close, try to develop a signalling system for those special times when you don't want to be interrupted. It could be as simple as a 'Do not disturb' sign. You can probably think of a more humorous and friendly way that fits your personality. Let your colleagues know what the signal is and use it when you need to.

When people break through your barrier, whether it's a closed door or your special signal, still greet them in a friendly manner. Explain to them that you need this undisturbed time and that you will deal with their matter later. Don't handle it immediately unless the interruption is genuinely warranted or people will know it's easy to get through and will do it again.

Are you the problem?

You also need to consider whether you are causing the problem yourself. People often enjoy and seek interruptions, particularly when they are procrastinating.

The other thing to check is whether your office layout is encouraging people to stop and talk with you. If people can catch your eye, they are more inclined to begin a conversation. Change the placement of your desk or strategically position a pot plant so that through traffic is not in your range of sight when you are working at your desk.

And, of course, if you are bad at following up people's requests, they will come back to disturb you again and again.

Being a good visitor

Being a good visitor yourself can help you to make better use of your time. Always remember that other people's time is as important to them as your time is to you, so be punctual. Think before you interrupt people who look as if they're concentrating, and make sure they are the right people to answer your question. Prepare beforehand so you can be brief. Ask if you can interrupt them and briefly state what you want. Schedule a later time if it is not convenient to discuss it now.

Over the next week

Before you choose your task for this week, decide whether the interruptions you are experiencing are of your own making; if they are, work out what you're going to do to change this. Otherwise, decide how you're going to give special care to your callers this week at the same time as handling their matters more quickly.

This week I will . . .

....

....

....

....

Daring to decide

Every decision carries an element of risk—it may prove to be a good decision but on the other hand it might turn out to be a bad decision. Some people hate that risk and would rather do anything than decide. Others ignore the risk and charge ahead regardless. Good decision-makers cover the risk by doing proper analysis and then making an informed decision.

Time-wasting decision making

In your concern to make only good decisions you may be wasting time getting bogged down with analysis. It's possible to gather too much information, to spend too much time on scrutiny and to waste time rechecking everything. When you overdo these things, you are actually displaying symptoms of procrastination. Check whether it's your negative, fearful or perfectionist streak coming out again (see Step 7).

And you can waste even more time feeling guilty when the outcome of one of your decisions is less than best. Sometimes this can cause so much distress that you adopt tactics to avoid personal responsibility for further decisions. The classic avoidance technique is to pass it on to a committee to decide, and that's an enormous time waster.

This is not to say that the other people who are affected by your decisions should not be involved in the decision-making process. If you don't involve them, your decisions may end up not being implemented, and that's just another waste of time.

Time-saving decision making

Time-saving decisions involve the right amount of research, the right amount of analysis and moving ahead with confidence together with those who are to implement your choice.

> **Steps for making a good decision**
> 1 Define the problem.
> 2 Collect information.
> 3 List and explore your alternatives.
> 4 Make a decision and then set it aside for a while.
> 5 Make your final decision and consider it closed.
> 6 Implement your decision.
> 7 Evaluate it.

What's the problem?

To make a good decision you must first of all know what you are supposed to be deciding on. So you should start by forming a clear picture of the problem.

Here are some questions to help you define the problem you have to resolve:

- What is the apparent issue that needs resolving?
- Do you suspect hidden issues are influencing the problem? How can you uncover these?
- Who is affected by it?
- Who is causing it?
- What will be the impact of making a decision?
- If I don't decide what will happen?
- What's the deadline for making this decision?

Making your decision

Now that you know what you are trying to decide, and when you need to decide by, you can begin collecting information to help you make a wise choice. Your time constraints and the potential impact of the decision will assist you in knowing how much time is reasonable to spend on this phase.

You must dig deeply enough to know that the facts you have gathered are correct without spending an inordinate amount of time on it.

Using a different source to cross-check your facts is a quick way to verify your information and give you greater confidence in your base data.

Once you have the base data you are ready to list possible solutions to your problem. When you are doing this, try to go beyond the obvious. It will help if you seek the opinion of others and consider their points of view.

Then begin exploring the impact of each solution. It may help to list the positive and negative aspects of each option. You won't want to jump to conclusions or display bias and favouritism in your choice, so try to be as objective as possible when doing this. If it's a close call, put a mathematical weighting on each positive and negative factor so that you can see which solution comes out ahead overall.

Now decide. It is often best to set the decision aside for a short while, or to sleep on it, so that any misgivings you might have about your choice can surface for your further consideration. But, remember, the objective of this is to make sure you have made a balanced and informed choice, it's not to send you into another phase of activity to justify putting off the decision.

Make your final decision and consider the matter closed. Don't allow it to cause you anxiety. Assure yourself that you have done your best with the time and information available to you.

Sometimes you will be obliged to make a quick interim or corrective decision. If so, go ahead in the knowledge that you may need to come back to it later for a strategic choice based on more thorough analysis. If you find you are making a lot of corrective decisions, get around to your strategic decision making sooner rather than later.

Making your decisions work

Your task is not over yet. You must ensure that the decision is implemented effectively. The way to do this is to get the involvement of the people who are affected by it. Explain why you have made your decision and tell them how you expect them to benefit from it. Discuss how they are affected and what you require them to do.

If you have been smart enough to enlist their support during the information-gathering process, this should be relatively easy. However, it is not always possible and decisions are not always palatable to those on the receiving end. This is where you need to exercise your best diplomacy. Encourage the participants to take the decision on board, even if only on trial, and agree to evaluate it a little further down the track. It's a good idea to evaluate decisions and their implementation, anyway, as part of your learning process and to help you make even better choices in the future.

Over the next week

When people are indecisive it makes life miserable for everybody. The number of emergency and panic decisions rises and these disrupt the smooth flow of your daily work. Managers in particular end up spending too much time sorting out problems. Avoid this by daring to decide this week.

This week I will . . .

....

....

....

....

Delegating duties

Believing that you're indispensable may give you a sense of importance and power but it won't do a thing for solving your time management problems. Taking on work assignments that belong to others and keeping the difficult jobs to yourself only loads your day with unnecessary tasks. And you are missing out on the joy and benefit of seeing others develop their skills and become part of an enthusiastic team.

Duties to delegate

Some types of activities are more easily delegated than others. Take a look at the list below and see whether any of the tasks on your schedule could be readily passed on to someone else.

Activities that can be easily delegated

- Routine activities.
- General tasks that don't require intimate company knowledge or specialist skills.
- Tasks for which specialist temporary assistants can be readily employed.
- Collection of data and fact finding.
- Problem analysis and preparation of possible solutions.
- Preparation of rough drafts.
- Smaller units of a bigger work assignment.
- Tasks that will develop and challenge other team members.

There may be aspects of your team's workload that can be more effectively outsourced. Consider the possibility of using service units both inside and outside your organisation as another way of off-loading routine work. As a simple example, instead of standing by a photocopy machine making multiple copies of a large document, send it out to a fast turnaround photocopying shop or your in-house copying service.

Another aspect of delegation is the opportunity to promote and develop other team members. If specialist skill is required, put a training program in place. Get the team together to discuss and plan their training needs and schedule practical application of their new skills soon after training. This can also be a good time to review systems and job responsibilities to ensure that the right people are doing the jobs and that there is no duplication of effort.

Why people don't delegate

When you read the list on page 83, did you find that you are doing jobs that could reasonably be done by others, jobs that they would enjoy and learn from? People give all kinds of excuses for not passing on their work to someone else. See whether any of these match your feelings or your reactions to the possibility of handing over some of your workload.

Why aren't you delegating?

- Impatience with the time others need to learn—I can do it quicker myself.
- A lack of acceptance of the way others work—I can do it better myself.
- Unwillingness to share the good work— I like doing that job and it's the only one I can pass on.
- A preference for 'hands-on' work—I'd rather be doing things than managing people.
- Inability to trust others—it's too risky to give it to someone else.
- An inflated ego—I'm the expert. I'm the only one who can do it.
- Insecurity—if I teach them I won't be needed any more.
- Poor management of resources—they're all too busy to take on extra work. I'll just have to work longer hours myself.

It's no good saying, 'The mess they made of things when I was on holiday is proof that they aren't up to it'. It was more likely proof that you have been keeping your work too close to yourself and not allowing others to learn and understand your systems.

How to delegate successfully

It's a special skill to be able to delegate successfully. Here are some of the steps you can take to ensure that any work you pass on is done well.

Set realistic assignments. Aim to give people activities that are within their current capability and training. The assignments can be difficult enough to challenge without being so unwieldy as to demoralise those who are trying to do them. Consider a gradual build-up of responsibility so the team gains confidence in their capability and you grow to trust in their ability. Get the team involved in defining the objectives so they are more motivated and accept ownership right from the start.

Give clear instructions. When you hand over an activity make sure that people understand exactly what they are required to do, what additional responsibilities you are giving to them and when you need the activity to be completed.

Agree on performance standards. You need the team's commitment to the activity and they need to know that it is achievable. Agree together on specific objectives and measures that will show the activity has been satisfactorily completed.

Establish checkpoints and reporting procedures. Setting checkpoints will help you to ensure that they stay on track, particularly when they are taking on a task for the first time. Discuss and agree on reasonable checkpoints and the reporting that is to be done for these checkpoints.

Establish its priority. Make sure the priority of this activity in relation to the team's other activities is understood and that any conflicts can be managed.

Make sure your people have the information, tools and equipment they need. You want them to be successful and you can't expect them to be so with inferior equipment or lack of information. If you usually make extensive use of personal contacts to get the job done, introduce them to those contacts. If you are on special mailing lists or have access to particular files, forward these on.

Delegate the authority too. Whatever authority you normally use and need to complete the activity should be delegated as well, otherwise they are going to have to keep coming back to you.

Encourage independence and creative thinking. Having assistants who are merely clones of yourself cuts off the possibilities that extra minds can bring to the activity. Wherever possible, delegate objectives rather than specific tasks so that your people have full creative control over how the objectives are achieved. If you are concerned they may go off at a tangent, use the checkpoint sessions to discuss options and approaches, and remember to keep an open mind when you do.

Support them in their efforts. When you hand over the task give your encouragement and support. Also be prepared to be available throughout the project to give a guiding hand and more encouragement when it is needed.

Demonstrate your trust in them. Let them get on with the activity without interference.

Give feedback. As the assignment progresses, give clear feedback on their progress so they are encouraged and can learn where adjustments are needed. And remember to let other people in the organisation know how important and useful the team is.

Time-wasting delegation

You are wasting your time delegating if you then loom over the hapless subordinates to maintain a detailed and vigilant watch over them.

The time-wasting delegator says:

- 'Do it how you like', and then insists on them doing it his or her way.
- 'I'm here if you need me', and then stifles them with help.
- 'You're in charge', and then steps in every time a decision has to be made.
- 'I'll let you work it out', and leaves them without the skills they need to do it.
- 'I have complete faith in your ability', and then keeps a constant check.
- 'I know it will take you a while to learn the ropes', and then expects perfection.

Force yourself to stay out of the activity loop, other than for agreed checkpoints. You will find that you not only have more time,

you will also have a more motivated and productive team.

When you are on the receiving end

When you're on the receiving end of delegated
duties, you can protect your time by applying some of the same ideas used for successful
delegation.

*Make sure that the assignment objectives are clear
and that you know by what measure your success
will be judged.* This is particularly important if
you have a manager who is inconsistent and
who changes course part-way through a project. Take notes during your meeting, read
back what you have written and, if necessary,
send a confirming memo so the details are
defined in writing.

Learn to say no. If it's not appropriate for you
to take on the assignment then don't accept
it. If it's your manager passing on the work,

discuss why it is not in line with your goals and priorities.

Where you see a potential conflict in your priorities, ask which activity you should put first. This is very important if you are taking on tasks from more than one person. If you don't feel you are able to negotiate the conflict yourself, ask for the two parties to resolve the matter at a management level. This is much better than accepting an unrealistic workload and not satisfying either demand.

Make sure that you will have access to all the resources you will need. Spend some time asking questions so that you know exactly what information is normally used to do the job. Ask to be given the delegated authority if it has not been passed to you.

Use the time you have together in checkpoint meetings wisely. Ask for specific checkpoints, particularly if the task is large. It is much better to be put back on track early in the project rather than after a large amount of work has been done. Plan ahead for these meetings so that they can be productive in moving you ahead. Prepare your report, present possible solutions, seek advice and guidance and ask for decisions to be made. Anticipate objections to the methods you have chosen to use and be prepared to defend them clearly and concisely.

Stand up for yourself when your manager interferes. Ask why this is happening and what you need to do for him or her to have confidence in your ability.

Remember your manager is human. Don't be too strident in your complaints and demands. Promote teamwork, ask for help so you can grow from the wisdom and knowledge of the group and don't have too high an opinion of your own ability.

Over the next week

Over the next week, look for ways to relieve your workload by sharing your knowledge and activities with others. If you have been putting up obstacles that have prevented this happening, try to remove them. Be prepared to invest a little time and effort today in developing other people for the benefit that you will all receive tomorrow.

This week I will . . .

....

....

....

....

REVIEW POINT

You are nearing the end of your 12-week plan.
Check that you have been keeping up with your
time-saving techniques and not letting bad
habits creep back in.

- Are the telephone, paperwork and meetings
  taking less time than they used to?

- Have you caught yourself procrastinating
  soon enough to fix the problem before the
  delay caused stress?

- Do you feel that you are dealing with callers
  more effectively now?

- Are you more decisive than you were a
  week ago?

- Can you still state what your goals are and
  do you consciously apply them to your
  work choices?

Looking for leverage

In Step 5 you looked at ways to clear the clutter around you. The purpose of this was to spend a little while organising things now so that you could file and find things more quickly and easily in the future. Because you file and retrieve documents over and over again, the small amount of effort expended now gives a handsome repeat return in the weeks and months that follow. This is called *leverage*, which in time management terms means using a little bit of time now to make a big time saving in the future.

Finding leverage

Here are examples of other activities that have high leverage:

- Undertaking training so that you can do tasks more quickly and easily.
- Training others so they can assist you.
- Delegating effectively to other people.
- Setting up systems so that you don't have to think each time.
- Improving and streamlining systems and procedures.
- Getting rid of unnecessary procedures.
- Building and maintaining relationships with people who can help you.

None of these things happen by themselves. You have to put in the effort now to get the future return. You need to seek out the high-leverage activities that you could do. Spend a little while thinking about what happens repeatedly in your working day. It might help to look back at your tracking chart (see Step 2). Zoom in on these specific problems and tasks and think of the things you could do that would eventually make them less demanding of your time.

Maybe you already know what could be done but you never seem to have time to get round to it. This is common. High-leverage activities tend to be long-term and are often in the non-urgent list, which you never reach. You must recognise the strategic importance of these tasks and raise their level of priority so that you can slowly chip away at them and gain the long-term benefit of your efforts.

Reusing the output of one task to help you complete a different task is another way of gaining leverage. Don't assume that everything has only one use. Before you set aside some work, stop and think whether this can be of further use to you or someone else.

Things that get in the way of high-leverage tasks

There are lots of things that can get in the way of doing high-leverage tasks but none more so than those that seem urgent. When an urgent interruption occurs, deal with it, then when the rush is over ask yourself, 'How can I stop this happening again?' There is probably some strategic high-leverage response that you can apply that will alleviate the problem or make it less disruptive in the future. Here are some other reasons why high-leverage activities don't get done:

Firefighting is fun. It gets your adrenalin pumping and gives you an immediate sense of reward when it is done. It's no wonder people favour these more urgent tasks rather than something slow and strategic. But if you want to make better use of your time you will have to forgo the firefighting habit.

Productivity tools that don't improve productivity. Some things that should be high leverage can actually get in the way of your productivity. For example, new computer systems and software should be making your job easier but, if you don't spend the time you need to learn how to use them properly, they will actually waste your time. Don't let machines manage you. Do what you have to do to master them.

Unquestioned processes and procedures. Procedures are usually put in place to streamline activities and smooth workflow. But when operating procedures become out of date or cumbersome they have the opposite effect. If this happens to you, be willing to break the rules.

Over the next week

What proportion of your week is usually spent on high-leverage activities? How much is spent on firefighting? Try to give an hour or more to at least one high-leverage task this week, and every week after this.

> This week I will . . .
>
> ....
>
> ....
>
> ....
>
> ....

Planning your daily schedule

A busy day doesn't have to be a stressful day. The secret of being busy without stress is to have control over how your day is spent. In the first 11 steps you have been taking action to gain more control over different aspects of your working day. In this step you will learn how to pull all those activities together into a daily plan, giving you better overall control.

If you have been working diligently on the previous steps you will be in very good shape to take on the challenge of daily planning. Daily planning does take quite a bit of discipline and organisation. However, once you are in the swing of it, it should take no more than ten minutes each day.

Making a master list

The first task is to make a master list of all the activities that you know you have to do now and in the near future. Forecast at least one month ahead; some people like to look out as far as three months.

List the routine activities you perform, the scheduled meetings, the big tasks that have a long lead time and the little tasks that you expect to finish in the next day or two. Try to make the list as complete as possible and try not to get too worried by its length.

If it is a recurring activity, like a monthly meeting, a weekly appointment or a daily task, indicate its recurrence period—month, week, day. If an activity has a completion deadline, put this date beside the activity.

As new activities arise, add them to your master list. Your master list will soon be an indispensable reminder of what has to be done and when it has to be done.

Estimating your time and deciding your priorities

To be fully effective the master list must be more than a simple to-do list. It should contain time estimates and priorities as well, so that you can actively plan your time, not just pick any activity from a list.

The ability to estimate accurately the time taken for tasks is an important skill that you should seek to develop. Poor estimation throws any schedule into chaos, and it is very demoralising when every day you don't get done what you had planned. This alone can be the source of many time management problems.

Make a rough estimate of the amount of time it will take to complete each activity. Remember to include planning, preparation and review time as well. Try to notice how long tasks take so that you can estimate better in the future.

Now take another look at your master list and decide on the importance of each task. For each task, indicate whether it:

- is important to your primary goals (see Step 1).
- is high leverage (see Step 11).
- could be delegated (see Step 10).
- is of routine or less importance.

While some tasks will become more urgent as they move closer to their deadline and must be included in your daily schedule, they may not be important in the overall scheme of things. Keeping an eye on the relative importance of your tasks will encourage you to concentrate on those things that matter and help you to rush through the less important things if necessary. It will also help you to schedule beneficial activities, like high-leverage tasks, which could otherwise slip by unattended because they are long-term.

Making a daily schedule

Start your daily planning by filling in the time slots for committed activities like meetings and other appointments. These are probably already listed in your appointment diary. You will also have a block of time (it should now be shorter) that you use for outgoing telephone calls and regular correspondence. Having a daily routine is useful as it encourages you to begin routine tasks without procrastination, and your schedule helps you to keep these activities to a reasonable time.

Next, scan your master list and identify tasks that you need to do today. Look for tasks that are nearing their deadline. Also, look ahead to find large tasks that you should begin well in advance of the deadline. When you are making your selections be keenly aware of your potential to procrastinate on certain tasks and make sure you don't allow this to happen.

Now, plan your activities for the day using the time estimates on your master schedule.

Your aim is to be effective, not simply busy, so balance those things that have become urgent with tasks that are important or of high leverage. Be ruthless in reducing the time spent on routine or unimportant tasks to make room in every day for important activities. Top performers attend to their high-priority tasks and are happy to put pressure on the rest.

A balanced schedule might include:

- two important or high-leverage tasks (3 hours)
- two or three tasks nearing deadline (1 hour)
- routine or less important tasks (45 minutes).

Notice that this appears to be a very short working day. This is because you should avoid tight scheduling. It is best to plan only 60 per cent of your day for concentrated tasks. This leaves you a buffer of 20 per cent for the unexpected. The other 20 per cent is for routine support activities, visitors, appointments, taking rest breaks and such.

Slot the top-priority tasks into the time of

day when you are most alert and have fewer interruptions. Fit the other items in your schedule around these and your fixed appointments.

Working your schedule

Try to work to your schedule. Force yourself to work within your estimated time limit, particularly when you are working on less important tasks, or if you are a poor-finishing procrastinator (see Step 7). Because you have planned for the unexpected there should be room for slippage without your whole day being thrown out. When a major disruption does occur, put the time you have left into the more important tasks and reduce the time spent on the others.

Use your schedule as your guide, not your obsession, and enjoy the satisfaction of crossing off each task as it is completed. Don't feel guilty if your schedule didn't work today. Begin each day anew with fresh enthusiasm.

Reviewing your schedule

Before you rush out at the end of the day, scan your schedule to find what was unfinished and needs to be transferred into tomorrow. If you find some task that is being repeatedly put off or not completed day after day, stop and decide why this is happening before moving it on again.

Ask these questions about tasks that are not getting done:

- Have you underestimated the time required for the task? For a task that you do regularly, time yourself. It will give you a better sense of time.

- Are you procrastinating? There may be something about the task that makes you put it off (review Step 7 for ideas on how to overcome this).

- Is it too early to start it? Maybe it's a task that needs more time for information to become available. Or maybe your creative energy needs to work on it in the background for a while longer. But make sure you aren't just procrastinating.

- Is it something you shouldn't be doing anyway? Either delegate it or cross it off your list and stop pretending you are going to do it, otherwise in a few months your master list will be totally unwieldy.
- Have you been forgetting things like travel time? Perhaps there are activities that actually happen in your day but which you are forgetting to account for in your schedule. If you suspect this, check it by redoing the tracking sheet (see Step 2).
- Are you trying to plan too much activity into your day? Or maybe you are letting comfortable and familiar tasks run overtime.

Every once in a while (say, quarterly) step back from your schedule and assess how your days are being spent. Your daily schedules will give you similar information to the tracking sheet you prepared at the beginning. It may be helpful to look over the chapters in this book again and decide whether any old or new time thieves have crept into your schedule. In particular, ask yourself whether your time allocations match your goals and whether your goals need adjustment.

Now close off your day and put yourself into a calm mood for an enjoyable evening.

Using an organiser

The planning method that has been described here can be implemented with your appointment diary, a notebook for your master list and a fresh piece of paper each day for your schedule. You may, however, prefer to use a personal organiser created especially for this purpose. These usually have loose-leaf pages for your schedules, a calendar, address book and other notes.

If you work at a computer regularly you may like the computerised organisers that can do a great job of managing your master list, posting appointments in your calendar, creating a daily schedule and even ringing an alarm when your next appointment is due. However, if you work away from your computer for part of the day you will have to be diligent in adding new tasks and appointments to your schedule when you return. A hand-held electronic diary and organiser may suit you better.

If you are using a computer system or other form of formal organiser, you may have to make adjustments to the planning method described here so as to fit in with their design. Either way, choose a method that you feel comfortable with and don't make it too complicated for yourself. It's possible to spend hours organising your organiser and not getting on with your job. Your organiser is meant to operate as a helpful assistant, not to become your master.

Over the next week

Planning your daily schedule is a skill, whether by the method described here or using a personal organiser. The learning curve can be rather long for cluttered people, so you will need to persevere with it for a while—but don't let that put you off getting started with it this week. Your daily schedule will become the best tool of all for managing your time.

This week I will . . .

....

....

....

....

REVIEW POINT

Congratulations, you have finished the 12 easy steps. Use this last review to set yourself up for ongoing success with managing your time.

- Did the goals you set in Step 1 turn out to be right for you? Make adjustments so they match your real priorities better.

- Is something still stealing too much time? Choose a different approach to try.

- Look at what you decided to do at the end of each step. List the successes you had, even if they are small, and enjoy a sense of achievement.

- Think about the benefits you have gained thus far. Use this as a reminder to keep on taking ownership of your time and reaping the rewards.

It's your time to use

The biggest time waster of all is an unwillingness to change. As you have read this book you have surely been encouraged to change some old time-wasting habits and been keen to introduce new time-saving ones. Changing entrenched work patterns is not always easy. That's why you have been taking it an easy step at a time, learning a new routine before moving onto the next.

You can keep building on the success of your new time management techniques by going back and giving extra ideas a try. But perhaps you have tried some of the ideas and feel that you have failed. Don't give up. Give them another go. Maybe you have been trying to change too many things at once, or need a little longer than a week to establish new behaviour patterns.

The more you believe that you can take control of your environment, the more effectively you will do so. Put some emotion into it. Be enthusiastic. Interestingly, without necessarily mentioning time management techniques, you will become a catalyst for change in those around you as you gain more control over how you use your time. In turn, this comes back to help you even more.

So, believe in yourself. It's your time to use and you can choose how you use it.